D1432269

Congratulations
+
Continued
success,

Ann Carlsen
+ John

On
Things
That Really
Matter

H. JACKSON BROWN, JR.

RUTLEDGE HILL PRESS®

NASHVILLE, TENNESSEE

Published in Nashville, Tennessee, by Rutledge Hill Press, Inc., 211 Seventh Avenue North, Nashville, Tennessee 37219.

Distributed in Canada by H.B. Fenn and Co., Ltd., 34 Nixon Road, Bolton, Ontario L7E 1W2. Distributed in Australia by The Five Mile Press Pty., Ltd., 22 Summit Road, Noble Park, Victoria 3174. Distributed in New Zealand by Southern Publishers Group, 22 Burleigh Street, Grafton, Auckland. Distributed in the United Kingdom by Verulam Publishing Ltd., 152a Park Street Lane, Park Street, St. Albans, Hertfordshire AL2 2AU.

Typography by Compass Communications, Inc., Nashville, Tennessee

Illustrations by Jim Hsieh

Book design by Harriette Bateman

ISBN: 1-55853-747-3

Printed in Hong Kong

1 2 3 4 5 6 7 8 9 — 04 03 02 01 00 99

INTRODUCTION

There is a fundamental question we all have to face. How are we to live our lives; by what principles and moral values will we be guided and inspired?

I once heard a minister compare life to a slippery staircase—an apt analogy. Slipping and sliding as we all do, we intuitively reach out for support, for anything to keep us from falling.

There is a handrail. But its stability is determined by the values we have chosen to guide our lives. It is, therefore, no stronger, no more reliable, than the quality of the choices we have made.

Is there a clear and simple way to decide which principles to embrace and which to reject? Using Immanuel Kant's proposition, which he called the *categorical imperative*, is one approach. In this method of determining the moral and ethical value of an act, one asks, "What would be the result

to humankind if everyone did it?"
For instance, what kind of world
would we have if everyone were
honest, self-disciplined, respon-
sible, kind, generous, courageous,
and virtuous? This is a question
that deserves serious reflection
and one you might use to examine
and challenge the things which
are important in your life.

Plato noted that the unex-
amined life is not worth living.
With that in mind, I dedicate this
book to all who seek a renewed
sense of moral clarity and
purpose.

We are all on the slippery stairs.
But our steps can be sure and steady
when we know our handrail is made
of sturdy stuff.

$\mathcal{T}$reasure the love you receive above all. It will survive long after gold and good health have vanished.

—Og Mandino

*B*e kinder than
necessary.

Make a rule and pray to God to help you keep it: never, if possible, lie down at night without being able to say, "I have made one human being a little wiser or a little happier or at least a little better this day."

—Charles Kingsley

$\mathscr{I}$'ve learned that . . .

. . . the person who is really
kind will never be alone or
unhappy. —Age 75

. . . I've never regretted the
nice things I've said about
people. —Age 38

I long to accomplish a great and noble task, but it is my chief duty to accomplish humble tasks as though they were great and noble. The world is moved along, not only by the mighty shoves of its heroes, but also by the aggregate of the tiny pushes of each honest worker.

—Helen Keller

Try measuring your wealth by what you are rather than by what you have. Put the tape measure around your heart rather than your bank account.

—Anonymous

$\mathcal{G}$ive life your best. You'll never regret it.

∾

$\mathcal{G}$et your priorities straight. No one ever said on his deathbed, "Gee, if I'd only spent more time at the office."

Fifty years from now, it will not matter what kind of car you drove, what kind of house you lived in, how much you had in your bank account, or what your clothes looked like. But the world may be a better place because you were important in the life of a child.

—Anonymous

I don't know what your destiny will be, but one thing I know: the only ones among you who will be really happy are those who will have sought and found how to serve.

—Albert Schweitzer

I've learned that . . .

. . . children want discipline
and guidelines because it
shows you care. —Age 32

. . . if you're too busy to do a
friend a favor, you're too busy.

—Age 39

Love is the only gold.

—Alfred, Lord Tennyson

❧

Children will not remember you for the material things you provided, but for the feeling that you cherished them.

—Gail Sweet

*D*ream big.
There is little power
in little plans.

It is not the critic who counts, not the man who points out how the strong man stumbles, or where the doer of deeds could have done them better. The credit belongs to the man who is actually in the arena, whose face is marred by dust and sweat and blood, who strives valiantly, who errs and comes short again and again, because there is no effort without error and shortcoming, but who does actually strive to do the deeds, who knows the great enthusiasms, the great devotions, who spends himself in a worthy cause, who best knows in the end the triumph of high achievement, and who at the worst, if he fails, at least fails while daring greatly, so that his place shall never be with those poor spirits who neither enjoy much nor suffer much because they live in the gray twilight that knows not victory nor defeat.

—Theodore Roosevelt

$\mathcal{G}$ive the utmost consideration to whom you marry. From this one decision will come 90 per cent of your happiness or misery.

∽

$\mathcal{L}$ive so that when your children think of fairness, caring and integrity, they will think of you.

*I hope I shall always possess
firmness and virtue enough to
maintain what I consider to be
the most enviable of all titles:
the character of an
"Honest Man."*

—George Washington

∾

*Things which matter most
must never be at the mercy of
things which matter least.*

—Johann Wolfgang von Goethe

EXCERPTS FROM

The Rockefeller Creed

I believe that every right
implies a responsibility; every
opportunity an obligation;
every possession a duty.

I believe that truth and
justice are fundamental to an
enduring social order.

I believe in the sacredness of
a promise, that a man's word

should be as good as his bond; that character—not wealth or power or position—is of supreme worth.

I believe that love is the greatest thing in the world; that it alone can overcome hate; that right can and will triumph over might.

I've learned that . . .

. . . children need loving the most when they are the hardest to love. —Age 79

. . . marriage is all about compromising and forgiving. —Age 35

*E*very person you meet knows something you don't know. Learn from them.

∿

*D*on't let the weeds grow around your dreams.

∿

*B*ecome someone's hero.

Do not pray for easy lives. Pray to be stronger men! Do not pray for tasks equal to your powers. Pray for powers equal to your tasks. Then the doing of your work will be no miracle, but you shall be the miracle.

—Phillips Brooks

$\mathcal{D}$onate two pints of blood
every year.

$\mathcal{S}$ign and carry your organ
donor card.

$\mathcal{C}$ommit yourself to constant
self improvement.

Let love be genuine; hate what is evil, hold fast to what is good; love one another with brotherly affection; outdo one another in showing honor. . . . *Rejoice in your hope, be patient in tribulation, be constant in prayer.*

—Romans 12:9-12 (RSV)

$\mathscr{I}$ve learned that . . .

. . . if you let your integrity slip just a little, it can have lasting consequences.

—Age 51

. . . a happy person is not a person with a certain set of circumstances but rather a person with a certain set of attitudes.

—Age 19

Do not consider anything for your interest which makes you break your word, quiet your modesty, or incline you to any practice which will not bear the light or look the world in the face.

—Marcus Aurelius

*G*et involved at your
child's school.

❧

*L*ove people more
than things.

❧

*L*et your life be your
sermon.

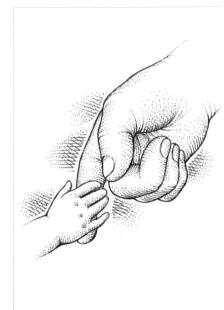

The most important handshake of your life will happen when your newborn infant's tiny hand grabs hold of your index finger.

—Anonymous

We are what we repeatedly do. Excellence then, is not an art but a habit.

—Aristotle

∿

He did it with all his heart, and prospered.

—2 Chronicles 31:21 (KJV)

*N*ever underestimate the influence of the people you have allowed into your life.

∽

*B*e happy with what you have while working for what you want.

∽

*L*ook for opportunities to make people feel important.

Many of the things you can count, don't count. Many of the things you can't count, really count.

—Albert Einstein

❧

You have a lifetime to work, but children are young once.

—Polish Proverb

$\mathcal{N}$ever give up on what you really want to do. The person with big dreams is more powerful than one with all the facts.

$\mathcal{L}$eave everything a little better than you found it.

*H*ave courage when things
go wrong.

∿

*W*hen a friend is in need,
help him without his having
to ask.

∿

*B*ecome the most positive
and enthusiastic person
you know.

Let your hand feel for the afflictions and distress of everyone, and let your hand give in proportion to your purse, remembering always the estimation of the widow's mite. Not everyone that asketh deserveth charity; all however, are worthy of the inquiry or the deserving may suffer.

—George Washington

A thousand words will not leave so deep an impression as one deed.

—Henrik Ibsen

❧

I agree . . . that there is a natural aristocracy among men. The grounds of this are virtue and talents.

—Thomas Jefferson

$\mathcal{B}$e open and accessible. The next person you meet could become your best friend.

∾

$\mathcal{N}$ever watch a video or movie with your children or take them to a live performance that involves activities and language that you don't want them to imitate.

Rotary International's Four-Way Test

1. Is it the TRUTH?

2. Is it FAIR to all concerned?

3. Will it build GOODWILL and BETTER FRIENDSHIPS?

4. Will it be BENEFICIAL to all concerned?

You are not here merely to make a living. You are here in order to enable the world to live more amply, with greater vision, with a finer spirit of hope and achievement. You are here to enrich the world, and you impoverish yourself if you forget the errand.

—Woodrow Wilson

That best portion of a good
man's life—
His little, nameless,
unremembered acts
Of kindness and of love.

—William Wordsworth

∽

Be ashamed to die until you
have won some victory for
humanity.

—Horace Mann

If we discovered that we had
only five minutes left to say all
that we wanted to say, every
telephone booth would be
occupied by people calling
other people to stammer that
they loved them.

—Christopher Morley

Never esteem anything as of advantage to you that will make you break your word or lose your self-respect.

—Marcus Aurelius

∞

Honor is like an island, rugged and without a beach; once we have left it, we can never return.

—Nicholas Boileau-Despreaux

I've learned that . . .

. . . pain is inevitable; misery is optional. —Age 100

. . . there's no greater resource when you're a new mother than your mother. —Age 29

Speak only well of people
and you'll never have
to whisper.

❧

Be modest. Much was
accomplished before you
were born.

❧

Never ignore evil.

He who passively accepts evil is as much involved in it as he who helps to perpetuate it.

—Martin Luther King Jr.

*R*emember that no situation is so bad that losing your temper won't make it worse.

∽

*A*pply this simple rule to your conversations: If you wouldn't write it down and sign it, don't say it.

Resolve to be tender with the young, compassionate with the aged, sympathetic with the striving, tolerant with the weak, and forgiving with the wrong. Sometime in your life you will have been all of these.

—Lloyd Shearer

Choose a charity in your community and support it generously with your time and money.

❧

Never deprive someone of hope; it might be all they have.

❧

Compliment three people every day.

$\mathcal{T}$ake care of your reputation;
it's your most valuable asset.

❧

$\mathcal{R}$egardless of the situation,
react with class.

❧

$\mathcal{C}$herish your children for
what they are, not for what
you want them to be.

$\mathcal{I}$'ve learned that . . .

. . . the older I get, the more I appreciate the times my parents said no.   —Age 17

. . . your conscience will sometimes hurt when everything else feels good.

—Age 52

This is our purpose: to make as meaningful as possible this life that has been bestowed upon us; to live in such a way that we may be proud of ourselves; to act in such a way that some part of us lives on.

—Oswald Spengler

*W*e—all of us, but especially the young—need around us individuals who possess a certain nobility, a language of soul, and qualities of human excellence worth imitating and striving for. Every parent knows this, which is why parents are concerned with both the company their children keep and the role models they choose. Children watch what we do as well as what we say, and if we expect them to take morality seriously, they must see adults taking it seriously.

—William J. Bennett

*R*ekindle old friendships.

❦

*N*ever underestimate the
power of a kind word or
deed.

❦

*S*hare your knowledge
and experience.

A happy home is a glimpse of heaven.

I've learned that . . .

. . . old friends and laugh
lines are life's finest trophies.

—Age 78

. . .an old Bible falling apart
usually belongs to someone
who isn't.　　　　—Age 62

21 Suggestions for Living Wisely and Well

1. Teach by example.

2. Bless every day with a generous act.

3. Never waste an opportunity to tell someone you love them.

4. Do something every day
that maintains your good
health.

5. Take family vacations
whether you can afford
them or not.

6. Stand up for your principles
even if you stand alone.

7. Judge your success by the degree that you're enjoying peace, health, and love.

8. Be there when people need you.

9. Be devoted to your spouse and dedicated to your children.

10. Be of service to your community and to your country.

11. Have courage when things go wrong.

12. Tell the truth.

13. Maintain a grateful heart.

14. Manage your resources wisely.

15. Don't overlook life's small joys while searching for the big ones.

16. Discover the power of prayer.

17. Discover the power of forgiveness.

18. Love people more than things.

19. Look for the good.

20. Search for the truth.

21. Hope for the best.

The people on our planet are not standing in a line single file. Everyone is really standing in a circle, holding hands. Whatever you give to the person standing next to you eventually comes back to you.

*R*emember that when you take inventory of the things in life you treasure most, you'll find that none of them was purchased with money.

$\mathcal{Y}$ou and I cannot determine what other men shall think and say about us. We can only determine what they ought to think of us and say about us.

—Josiah Gilbert Holland

∽

$\mathcal{A}$ reputation for a thousand years may depend upon the conduct of a single moment.

—Ernest Bramah

I've learned that . . .

. . . a torch loses no heat by lighting a thousand torches.

—Age 59

. . . people will remember how you treated them long after they have forgotten what you were wearing.   —Age 42

$\mathcal{D}$on't forget that what you
are thinking about,
you are becoming.

∾

$\mathcal{W}$hen facing a difficult task,
act as though it is impossible
to fail. If you're going after
Moby Dick, take along the
tartar sauce.

Do not care overly much for wealth or power or fame, or one day you will meet someone who cares for none of these things, and you will realize how poor you have become.

—Rudyard Kipling

I would like to have engraved inside every wedding band Be kind to one another. This is the Golden Rule of marriage and the secret of making love last through the years.

—Rudolph Ray

∾

In matters of style, swim with the current; in matters of principle, stand like a rock.

—Thomas Jefferson

*L*et your children observe
you being generous to those
in need.

❧

*N*ever be too busy to meet
someone new.

❧

*R*emember that every day
we have the power to
do good by words if not
by deeds.

A man's accomplishments in life are the cumulative effect of his attention to detail.

—John Foster Dulles

∾

T reat people as if they were what they ought to be and you can help them to become what they are capable of becoming.

—Johann Wolfgang von Goethe

$\mathcal{I}$ve learned that . . .

. . . I don't need more to be thankful for; I need to be thankful more. —Age 46

. . . when someone forgives you, they give you a gift; when you forgive someone else, you give a gift to yourself. —Age 32

What is the use in living if not to strive for noble causes and to make this muddled world a better place for those who will live in it after you are gone?

—Winston Churchill

$\mathcal{B}$ecome an example of
what you want to see more of
in the world.

∿

$\mathcal{R}$emember that no one
deserves your best behavior
more than your family.

*E*xercise caution in your business affairs for the world is full of trickery. But let this not blind you to what virtue there is. Many persons strive for high ideals and everywhere life is full of heroism. . . .

You are a child of the universe, no less than the trees and the stars; you have a right to be here. And whether or not it is clear to you, no doubt the universe is unfolding as it should.

Therefore, be at peace with God, whatever you conceive Him to be, and whatever your labors and aspirations in the noisy confusion of life, keep peace with your soul.

With all its sham, drudgery, and broken dreams, it is still a beautiful world. Be careful. Strive to be happy.

—Anonymous

It is one of the most beautiful compensations of life that no man can sincerely try to help another without helping himself.

—Ralph Waldo Emerson

$\mathcal{I}$'ve learned that . . .

. . . the best way to have
friends is to be the kind of
friend you'd like to have.

—Age 62

. . . love never grows old
when you grow old with the
one you love.   —Age 71

When you were born, you cried and the world rejoiced. Live your life in such a manner that when you die the world cries and you rejoice.

—Old Indian Proverb

*R*emember that you can almost always improve your performance by improving your attitude.

❧

*B*e bold and courageous. When you look back on your life, you'll regret the things you didn't do more than the ones you did.

$\mathcal{I}$'ve learned that . . .

. . . if you want your children to be good readers, let them see you read. —Age 31

. . . the quality of my life is enhanced by volunteering.

—Age 36

$\mathcal{N}$ever resist a
generous impulse.

The real things haven't
   changed.
It is still best to be honest and
   truthful;
to make the most of what we
   have;
to be happy with simple
   pleasures;
and to have courage when
   things go wrong.

—Laura Ingalls Wilder

How wonderful it is that nobody need wait a single moment before starting to improve their world.

—Anne Frank

∾

Remember the three powerful resources you always have available to you:

LOVE

PRAYER

FORGIVENESS

$\mathcal{L}$ove, respect, and home-grown tomatoes are all that really matter in the end.

—Robert Waller

*P*lant more flowers than
you pick.

&

*F*ollow your own star.

&

*R*emember the ones who
love you.